DARING WOMEN

25 WOMEN WHO DARED *to* CREATE

by Rebecca Stanborough

COMPASS POINT BOOKS
a capstone imprint

Daring Women is published by Compass Point Books, an imprint of Capstone.
1710 Roe Crest Drive
North Mankato, Minnesota 56003
www.capstonepub.com

Library of Congress Cataloging-in-Publication Data is available on the Library of Congress website.
ISBN: 978-0-7565-6617-3 (hardcover)
ISBN: 978-0-7565-6661-6 (paperback)
ISBN: 978-0-7565-6625-8 (eBook PDF)

Summary: Discover 25 women who designed their own futures. From dancers to musicians to artists, these women drew from their imaginations and dreamed of the impossible.

Image Credits
Alamy: History and Art Collection, 7; Art Resource: Smithsonian American Art Museum, Washington, DC, 11; Bridgeman Images: Collection Gregoire, 19; Getty Images: Andrew Aitchison, 15, Anthony Barboza, 37, Bettmann, 9, Cem Ozdel/Anadolu Agency, 48, Hansel Mieth/The LIFE Picture Collection, 21, Hulton Deutsch, 35, Jeremy Chan, 47, Jeremy Sutton-Hibbert, 13, JOCHEN LUEBKE, 53, Leigh Vogel, 55, Lester Cohen, 31, Michael Ochs Archives, 33, Nickolas Muray, 27, SHAUN CURRY, 57; Granger: Cover, 43; Library of Congress Prints and Photographs Division: 17, 22, 25; Newscom: View Pictures/Anthony Weller, 51; Shutterstock: Cryptographer, 5, GrislyFrank, 41; Tinseltown, 39; Wikimedia: Library of Congress, 29, U.S. Army Official Photograph, 45

Design Elements by Shutterstock

Editorial Credits
Editors: Peter Mavrikis and Mari Bolte; Designer: Bobbie Nuytten;
Media Researcher: Tracy Cummins; Production Specialist: Laura Manthe

Printed in the United States of America.
PA117

— TABLE OF CONTENTS —

INTRODUCTION

Great art changes the world, even when the world does not want to change. Great art tells the truth. It kindles joy. It bears witness to history. And it expresses passion in all its forms.

This book celebrates the work of women artists around the globe. This is how they changed the world: with brush and canvas, bronze and clay, needle and thread, music and movement, lens and light, brick and blueprints. Our world is better because these wonderous workers dared to pursue their dreams and create beautiful and powerful works of art.

> *Do your work and don't let anyone or anything stop you. Don't do your work to please other people; do it to please yourself.*
>
> —Faith Ringgold, painter

Women artists challenge themselves creatively, through song, dance, sculpture, photography, painting, architecture, and other forms of art.

Chapter 1

BRUSH AND CANVAS

Women have been painting fine art for centuries. A mere 50 years after Michelangelo painted the Sistine Chapel in 1508, Plautilla Nelli created a nearly life-size painting of *The Last Supper*. In the mid-1600s, when Rembrandt was creating masterworks like *The Night Watch* in Holland, Rachel Ruysch was painting exquisite still lifes for clients throughout Europe. Yet art history books failed to include most of the women who painted in the Italian Renaissance and the Dutch Golden Age.

The painters discussed here were fortunate. Though many of them had to defy society's expectations to create art, they were working in the 20th and 21st centuries. The century that brought women the right to vote also brought new opportunities to create art with brush and canvas.

Georgia O'Keeffe
(1887–1986)

A young Wisconsin girl named Georgia O'Keeffe picked up a brush. She began painting the natural world around her. She painted her way into art schools in Chicago and New York, spending years imitating the style of master painters.

Georgia O'Keeffe is recognized by many as the "Mother of American Modernism." She is best known for her paintings of natural objects such as enlarged flowers, leaves, and natural landscapes.

"But it was all academic," she remembered. "We were taught to paint like somebody else. It made me not want to paint at all." For a while, she laid down her paintbrush.

Then she discovered the work of Arthur Dow, whose idea was to "fill a space in a beautiful way." She began painting in a bold, colorful, abstract style that enhanced what she saw in the natural world. She painted everything from flowers to skyscrapers in a daring, modernist style.

In 1929, O'Keeffe spent a summer in Ghost Ranch, New Mexico. She went looking for flowers to paint, but what she found instead were bleached animal bones. She loved their shapes. She painted them larger than life and often centered them over the desert horizon.

O'Keeffe made New Mexico her home in 1949. She would get up at 7 a.m. and drive her Model A Ford out across the countryside. She had removed the back seat so she could paint in the car, which gave her some relief from the fierce desert heat. People who knew her well said she loved working in New Mexico because she could be alone there.

President Gerald Ford awarded Georgia O'Keeffe the Presidential Medal of Freedom in 1977. Today, she is considered one of the most important American painters of the 20th century.

O'Keeffe once compared the life of an artist to walking on a knife's edge. "So what? So what if you fall off? I'd rather be doing something I really wanted to do," she said.

In 2014, O'Keeffe's *Jimson Weed/White Flower No. 1* sold for $44.4 million. It was the most expensive painting ever sold by a woman artist. The highest sale price of a painting by a male artist is Leonardo da Vinci's *Salvator Mundi*. It sold in 2017 for $450.3 million.

Frida Kahlo
(1907-1954)

La Casa Azul, or "The Blue House," is a museum in Mexico City dedicated to Frida Kahlo. People come from all over the world to see and learn what life was like for the famous artist. As a child, Frida was surrounded by pets, including cats, dogs, monkeys, and even a deer. Her father was a photographer and painter. He brought Kahlo along to see the Mexican countryside documenting their culture.

When Kahlo was six years old, she contracted polio, a disease that twisted her pelvis and thinned her right leg. At age 18, her school bus was struck by an electric streetcar. Her spine was broken in three places. Her leg and foot were shattered, and a handrail pierced her abdomen. Kahlo was in the hospital for more than a year. There, she began painting in earnest. Her mother brought in a mirror and hung it above her so Kahlo could paint self-portraits.

Frida Kahlo worked on hundreds of paintings, including this portrait of a wealthy San Francisco society woman in 1931.

She kept painting self-portraits—and having painful surgeries—for the rest of her life. Her art frequently explored her physical suffering.

Early in her career, her work was often overshadowed by the paintings and sculptures of her husband, Diego Rivera. The two were famous for their parties and for the ups and downs of their relationship. But in time, she made a name for herself.

In her self-portraits, Kahlo is often adorned in flowers and dressed in traditional Tehuana clothing. She is sometimes surrounded by birds and animals like the ones at La Casa Azul. Sometimes she appears to be floating. Other times she is confined to hospital beds.

Though she only lived to be 47 years old, Frida Kahlo became a leading figure in the Mexican surrealist tradition. Her face—that frank stare beneath the dark eyebrows—is instantly recognizable. Despite the many hardships she endured, she insisted on free self-expression.

Alma Thomas
(1891–1978)

When Alma Thomas was a girl, she dreamed of being an architect—a nearly impossible dream at the time. Few women would have considered taking a career in a male-dominated field, especially when women were not allowed to handle a voting ballot, let alone a blueprint.

Instead of studying architecture, she studied art. Alma Thomas became the first student to graduate from the newly formed art department at Howard University, a historically black university. After obtaining a master's degree, she taught art to junior high school children for 38 years. She was such a devoted teacher that she wasn't able to give her own art the time it deserved.

Finally, when she retired from the classroom in 1960, she turned to her own canvases. She began developing the abstract, colorful style for which she is known today.

Thomas was part of a group of painters known as the Washington Color School. Her work is known for its tightly packed, abstract pats of color that seem to move on their own across the canvas. Some paintings look like mosaics. Some look rain-streaked.

"Color is life," Thomas said. "Light is the mother of color. Light reveals to us the spirit and living soul of the world through colors."

In 1972, Thomas was the first black woman to have a solo exhibition at New York City's Whitney Museum of American Art. Three of her works were chosen by First Lady Michelle Obama to hang in the White House. In 2015, her painting *Resurrection* was displayed publicly in the White House. It was the first piece by an African American woman to be placed as a permanent part of the White House collection.

Thomas remains an inspiration to many, not only because she developed her own bold style in an era when race and gender limited her opportunities, but because she accomplished so much so late in her life.

Alma Thomas posed in front of one of her paintings in 1976.

She once told a reporter, "One of the things [black people] couldn't do was go into museums, let alone think of hanging our pictures there. Look at me now."

The Washington Color School was not an actual school. It was a group of artists in the 1950s and 1960s who experimented with painting in large patterns of attention-grabbing color.

MOTHERS BUILDING: MOSAICS AND MURALS BY WPA ARTISTS

During the Great Depression, the U.S. government paid people to create public art through the Works Progress Administration (WPA). The Mothers Building at the San Francisco Zoo is home to several of these works. Three sisters, Helen, Margaret, and Ester Bruton, created large mosaics from tile pieces. Their paintings depict scenes of animals and children.

The building also houses two huge egg tempera murals by Helen Forbes and Dorothy Pucinelli. They show scenes from the biblical story of Noah's Ark. Over the years, salt air and water have damaged the artworks. The Mothers Building also needs repairs. It is closed until funds can be raised to restore it.

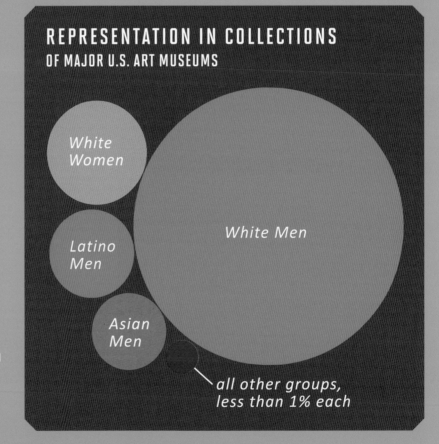

REPRESENTATION IN COLLECTIONS
OF MAJOR U.S. ART MUSEUMS

White Women

White Men

Latino Men

Asian Men

all other groups, less than 1% each

Yayoi Kusama

(1929–)

When Yayoi Kusama was 10, she began seeing things. Pumpkins and flowers spoke to her. She painted the strange things she saw. She called it "art-medicine." She wanted to become a painter. Her mother wanted her to marry and settle down. They fought every day.

As soon as she could, Kusama traveled to New York City. It was the epicenter of art in the 1960s, and Kusama desperately wanted to succeed. It was not easy. She was so poor that some days she could not afford to buy food. Her bed was a discarded door she had found on the street.

She painted all day long and into the night. Eventually, she connected with some of the most famous pop artists in New York City. This led to her own art show.

Yayoi Kasama is the top-selling living female artist in the world. In 2014, her pieces sold at auction totaled more than $34 million.

Her paintings were made up of thousands of polka dots. She called the endless dots "infinity nets." The repetitive dots made Kusama feel connected to the universe and calmed her anxiety. She painted canvases, walls, fabrics, and even people. In her mirror rooms, dots were

In 1957, Kusama wrote a letter to Georgia O'Keeffe, expressing her wish to come to the United States. O'Keeffe wrote back. That letter was the first of several that inspired Kusama to make the trek across the ocean.

painted on floors, ceilings, and mirrors made the rooms seem to go on forever.

"Our Earth is only one polka dot among a million stars in the cosmos. Polka dots are a way to infinity," Kusama said.

Although her unusual ideas brought her a measure of fame, Kusama struggled to find financial success in New York. She was especially discouraged when her more famous friends—artists such as Andy Warhol—copied her ideas.

In 1973, Kusama moved back to Japan. In addition to her financial hardships, she struggled with mental illness. Her doctor diagnosed her with schizophrenia related to childhood trauma. Today, Kusama lives in a facility where she can get help with her mental illness. Her studio is across the

According to *The Art Newspaper*, only one of the top 20 most-visited exhibitions in the world was headlined by a woman in 2017: Yayoi Kusama's "My Eternal Soul" at Tokyo's National Art Center.

street. In 2017, the Yayoi Kusama Museum opened in Tokyo. Her special polka dots are more popular now than ever.

Lubaina Himid
(1954–)

When Lubaina Himid and her mother went shopping, they were on the lookout. Each trip was like an expedition, spent searching for color, patterns, and designs that showed up on what people wore.

"My mother was a textile designer and so, because we looked at beautiful things in shops and in art museums when I was a child, the idea of being an artist was always a possibility in my mind," Himid says.

But she quickly realized that she was not seeing black people represented in artwork. Along with other artists in the 1980s and 1990s, Himid became part of the British Black Arts Movement.

Himid's bold, colorful paintings have sought to reveal the lives and experiences of people who have been left out of

Lubaina Himid's Jelly Mould Pavilion is a full-sized model of the ceramic jelly moulds the artist collected over her lifetime.

history books and art museums. For a 2004 installation called *Naming the Money*, Himid created 100 life-size wooden cutouts. Each figure had an original African name and occupation, along with a name given by enslavers. In another recent exhibition, Himid painted over newspaper headlines and photographs to recast the way images of black people were presented.

"If you don't see yourself on the TV, in the art gallery, or in the newspapers in any form except as a criminal, then that's hard," Himid has been quoted as saying. "If you're creative then you try to make or sing or build your way out of that."

Himid has focused much of her energy on promoting the artwork of other women of color. In 2017, she won the Turner Prize, one of the United Kingdom's highest art awards. In 2018, she was appointed CBE (Commander of the Most Excellent Order of the British Empire) for her services to art.

Chapter 2

BRONZE AND CLAY

In the Swabian Jura region of southern Germany, archaeologists have found some of the oldest examples of artwork on Earth. More than 50 small sculptures have been discovered, including lions, mammoths, and even a female figure the archaeologists have named the Venus of Hohle Fels. Many of the figurines are 40,000 years old. No one knows who the artists were.

The women discussed here sculpted with clay, bronze, plaster, wood, and many other materials. They are part of one of the most ancient traditions on Earth.

Nampeyo
(1860–1942)

Like many Tewa mothers living on First Mesa in New Mexico, White Corn placed a lump of clay in her daughter Nampeyo's hands. This simple act was the beginning of Nampeyo's life as an artist.

Growing up among Hopi neighbors, Nampeyo learned to make pots at a young age. Her family used those pots for ceremonial and household purposes.

Pottery requires a lot of water. Even today, parts of First Mesa have no running

Nampeyo never learned how to write, so her pottery was never signed.

water. Nampeyo had to walk to fill a large canteen called an *olla* with spring water. A sling that ran across her forehead and down her back helped her haul the heavy water. The olla was coated with pitch, a thick, black substance that kept the water from seeping out.

Nampeyo also needed clay. She dug it up out of the ground. Then she worked it with her feet and hands to remove any pebbles. Once it was smooth, she coiled it round and round, stopping to even out the pot with a melon rind. When the pot was the right shape—round and deep—she surrounded it with sheep dung and bones and placed it on a low fire.

After her pottery had fired for a day, it could be painted. She decorated pottery with black, boiled beeweed and other natural pigments. She used patterns she had seen on shards of ancient pottery found near the mesa.

Nampeyo once told a translator, "When I first began to paint, I used to go to the ancient village and pick up pieces of pottery and copy the designs. That is how I learned to paint. But now I just close my eyes and see designs and I paint them."

Nampeyo's art became incredibly popular among collectors. Before, people who were not indigenous saw traditionally made Hopi pots as simple souvenirs. Nampeyo's artistry helped them see that the pottery was much more important. She became a kind of icon of the American West. Her photograph appeared on travel brochures. Her pottery, though never signed, sold all over the United States. Even more importantly, she taught her techniques to other First Mesa artists.

She inspired generations of her relatives to carry on the pottery-making tradition. Her artworks appear in museums around the country, including the Smithsonian Institution's Museum of the American Indian.

Camille Claudel
(1864–1943)

For Camille Claudel, the best thing in Villeneuve, the French village where she grew up, was its red, dense clay used to make roof tiles. But Claudel baked that red clay into terracotta figures. They were so lovely that her art teachers gasped and marveled.

No matter how good her figures, though, many people in the late 1800s believed that women should not pursue art. Being a female sculptor was especially taboo. Women were not supposed to study the nude human form. Even though male artists did it all the time, it was not considered proper for women. In time, however, Claudel and her teachers persuaded her father to allow her to study art in Paris, at the Academie Colarossi.

Claudel studied intensely. She was such a talented student that one of her mentors, Auguste Rodin, took a special interest in her work. Rodin was one of the most

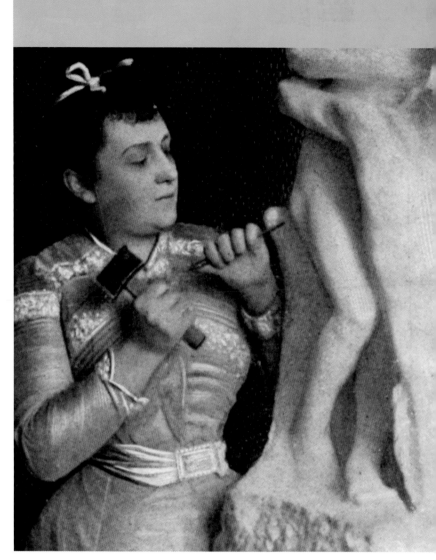

Camille Claudel in 1903

popular sculptors in Europe. Soon, the two were involved romantically and artistically. In the late 1880s and early 1890s, Claudel produced sculptures of such great quality that people didn't believe they could have been made by a woman. Instead, Rodin was credited.

Some of her work—especially *L'Abandon* and *Sakuntala*—attracted critics. People did not think a woman should sculpt male and female bodies together. Rodin's similar sculptures were never challenged.

When the relationship with Rodin ended, Claudel plunged into a period of sorrow. Her mother and brother had never approved of her art career or her relationship. They had her committed to an asylum. Claudel's friends insisted she was not insane. Doctors wrote letters pleading for her release. But her family would not let her be free. She remained in the asylum, unable even to receive letters, for 30 years until her death at age 78.

Claudel destroyed many of her own works after she left Rodin. Fewer than 100 survived. Today, her sculptures are highly sought after. In 2017, a rare collection once owned by Claudel's sister was put up for sale. The 20 works brought in $4.1 million.

Augusta Savage
(1892–1962)

One of the Bible's Ten Commandments forbids the making of "graven images." Some take this to mean any object carved or shaped that could be worshiped. For Edward Fells, a minister in Green Cove Springs, Florida, that meant his daughter's red clay sculptures were not allowed. "My father," Augusta Savage said, ". . . almost whipped all the art out of me."

Almost.

Savage moved to New York City during the Harlem Renaissance, a period when African American art, music, and literature were thriving nationwide. She studied at Cooper Union School of Art. She created busts of well-known African Americans such as W.E.B. DuBois. One of her sculptures, *Gamin*, depicted her young cousin Ellis. It was so striking that it won her a scholarship to study at the Académie de la Grande Chaumière in Paris. But when the French government learned she was black, they took away the scholarship. In a bold move, Savage went public.

Eventually, she made it to Paris. She studied with well-known artists and had an exhibition of her own work.

In 1932, Savage returned to New York. She opened the Savage Studio of Arts & Crafts. It was the first gallery owned by an African American woman in the United States. She gave free art lessons to people in her community. She helped train artists including Jacob Lawrence and Gwendolyn Knight, who would become important painters in their own right.

Savage was invited to create a sculpture for the 1939 World's Fair. It would celebrate African American music. After two years of work, *The Harp* was finished. The 16-foot (5-meter)-tall work of art showed the arm of God supporting a choir of singers whose robes made up the harp strings. *The Harp* was admired by millions who

Augusta Savage working on one of her sculptures in her studio in Harlem, New York, 1938

attended the exhibition—but like many of the other works created for the fair, it was destroyed when the fair ended because there was nowhere to store it.

Today, Augusta Savage is considered one of the most influential artists of the 20th century. Her art lives on through her own work, as well as the work of her students.

Few of Augusta Savage's artworks have survived, but *Gamin* is part of the Smithsonian Institution's collection.

Marisol Escobar

(1930–2016)

Marisol had a habit of keeping silent. It began at the age of 11, after her mother's suicide. Much later, she used silence to create a sense of mystery.

Marisol Escobar was born in Paris, France. Her family was from Venezuela, in South America. The Escobars often traveled between the two countries. Her father moved them to Los Angeles in 1946. Marisol returned to Paris in 1949 to study. Afterward, she took art classes in New York City and Provincetown, Rhode Island.

She began sculpting to cheer herself up.

Marisol Escobar examining a sculpture by artist Henry Moore at a New York City gallery, 1963.

"I was very sad myself, and the people I met were so depressing," she explained. "I started doing something funny so I would be happier—and it worked."

In 1962, her first New York City show

opened to instant acclaim. Her sculptures of friends and famous people were funny, boxy, and bright. Marisol worked found objects and fabric into the compositions. At shows in 1964 and 1966, thousands of people lined up to see her work. Magazines profiled her. Pop artist Andy Warhol put her in his films.

In response to her fame, Marisol disappeared. She would take sudden trips to distant parts of the world. Art dealers were furious. Marisol came back only when she was ready.

She was an expert at creating mystery. Once, she appeared at a press conference where several artists were being interviewed. She wore a white mask over her face. When the audience demanded that she take off the mask, she tugged a string and it fell away—but she had painted her face to match the mask.

Marisol went on making pop art well into the 1980s. Her art remained both playful and political. She sculpted a series of sea creatures that all had her face. She also sculpted migrant workers and poor Cuban children—groups that were overlooked by society. Though her style went in and out of favor, she continued to carve bold, chunky sculptures out of wood. She created a large version of herself studying Leonardo da Vinci's *The Last Supper*. That self-portrait is now part of the Metropolitan Museum of Art's collection, located in New York City.

At the time, pop art was dominated by men. Marisol was one of the few women who stood out. The Albright-Knox Art Gallery was the first gallery to buy one of her sculptures. When she died, she left the gallery her entire estate.

Chapter 3

MUSIC AND MOVEMENT

In 2019, two months before she won five Grammy awards, Billie Eilish said, "All anybody wants to talk about is me. Nobody really talks about the music."

For much of music and dance history, women composers and choreographers broke tradition. They were so unusual that people wanted to talk about their gender instead of their art.

Amy Beach
(1867–1944)

Clara Cheney sang to her two-year-old daughter, Amy, as she rocked her to sleep. Amy sang back, improvising the alto harmony to her mother's melody.

So began the life of composer Amy Cheney Beach. Young Amy composed her first song—"Mama's Waltz"—at age four. She learned to play piano at six. By 17, she was performing with the world-renowned Boston Symphony Orchestra.

Amy married Dr. Henry Beach, a doctor at Harvard Medical School. He encouraged her musical work in many ways, but he was what Beach called "old-fashioned." For example, he asked that she limit the number of her public performances and donate her earnings to charity. And he did not want her to study in Europe, as many male composers did.

Amy Beach was one of the most well-respected composers of her time, and she achieved all her success without any formal training.

Instead, Beach studied on her own. "I have never gone to a concert hall simply for enjoyment or pastime; I have always tried to study the works. . . . When I got home, then, I would sit down and write out the themes I could remember, with their proper instrumentation. Then I compared my work with the score."

Beach's work was praised by audiences. But some critics struggled with what a woman's music should sound like. They said her compositions should be gentle and melodic instead of bold. One critic even wrote, "There is nothing feminine about the writing; all her work is strong and brilliant."

Amy Beach's *Gaelic Symphony,* performed by the Boston Symphony Orchestra in 1896, was the first symphony ever written and published by an American woman.

Beach's career was long and productive. She composed more than 150 individual songs, plus many large-scale works. She wrote symphonies, concertos, choral works, chamber music, and an opera. She also used her prominence to advance the careers of other women in music.

"One thing I have learned from my audiences is that young women artists and composers shouldn't be afraid to pitch right in and try," she said.

Martha Graham
(1894–1991)

Martha Graham balanced on a stack of books. She strained to look down at a drop of water glistening on a glass slide.

"What do you see?" her father asked.

"Pure water," she told him. Then he showed her the slide under a microscope. There were microbes wiggling in the water!

"You must look for the truth," her father told her, "good, bad, or unsettling." Years later, she called this moment her "first dance lesson." It wasn't her last, though. Graham went on to become one of the most influential dancers and choreographers of the 20th century. Her work is celebrated for the truths she revealed through movement.

Graham spent her early years studying and dancing with Ruth St. Denis and Ted Shawn at the Denishawn company. She also began to experiment and create her own choreography. In 1926, she formed a dance company, the Martha Graham School for Contemporary Dance.

Her first piece of choreography shocked audiences who were used to soft and delicate ballets. Reviewers described Graham's movements as angular, sharp, and even ugly. Some audiences booed. To many, though, Graham's choreography was intensely beautiful. Dancers lean dangerously, cradle each other, press outward with their heels. They tremble, stutter, and even sit on each other like furniture.

In 1998, Martha Graham was given the title "Dancer of the Century."

Graham created 181 ballets over nearly 70 years. Her ballets celebrated the lives of all kinds of women, from Greek goddesses to pioneer housewives. Joan of Arc, Emily Dickinson, and the mythical Clytemnestra were all subjects.

In 1937, she was invited to the White House by President Franklin D. Roosevelt. She was the first dancer to perform there. In 1976, President Gerald Ford awarded her the nation's highest civilian honor, the Presidential Medal of Freedom with Distinction.

Martha Graham is often called the mother of modern dance. She is credited with inventing a whole new vocabulary for dancing. But she did not believe in competing with other creators.

> "You are in competition with one person only, and that is the individual you know you can become."
> —Martha Graham

Katherine Dunham
(1909–2006)

Katherine Dunham was only three years old when her mother died. Her father sent her to live with her aunt on the south side of Chicago. There, she met Clara Dunham and a full cast of uncles and aunts who performed in vaudeville theater productions. At the time, vaudeville was the only kind of theater that accepted black performers.

As Dunham got older, she knew she wanted to dance. She had studied ballet growing up and was drawn to the formality of it, but she also longed to express something else. She was part of a movement in college known as the New Negro Movement. It was a group of intellectuals who wanted to use art to fight racial prejudice. In 1930, Dunham formed the Ballet Negre, the first African American ballet company in the nation.

Dunham wanted to explore cultural roots of the African diaspora as a way of defining a new African American identity. She traveled to Haiti, Jamaica, Martinique, and Trinidad to study dance as an anthropologist. She published *Journey to*

Katherine Dunham was inspired by African, African American, Caribbean, and South American dance styles.

Accompong and other books that compiled her research.

In the late 1930s, she formed the Katherine Dunham Dance Company. Her choreography used the dance forms she had learned abroad. She staged more than 100 pieces. Her style helped develop an entirely new set of modernist dance techniques that are still taught today.

Dunham and her dance company dazzled audiences worldwide. They performed on Broadway in New York City and in many films. But when the company traveled in the U.S., they faced severe discrimination. Dunham fought back by refusing to perform in theaters where black and white patrons had to sit separately. She sued to protect her civil rights and walked out on movie deals if her dancers weren't treated with respect.

Throughout her long career, Katherine Dunham used dance to help people. She founded performing arts schools in Chicago, New York, East St. Louis, and in Haiti to uplift communities there. And she used her

Modernism is an artistic movement that began in the late 1800s and continued through the 1970s. Modern artists often rejected realistic depictions. They experimented with forms, lines, and materials that overturned tradition.

fame to bring attention to important causes, once going on a 47-day hunger strike to protest the unfair deportation of Haitian immigrants.

As a researcher, author, choreographer, educator, and powerhouse celebrity, Katherine Dunham's impact on modern dance is unequaled.

Tania León
(1943–)

When Tania León was just 23 years old, she had to make a tough choice: Stay with her family in Cuba, or leave them behind to study music in America. Traveling to the United States was a long shot. She would have to win a spot on a Freedom Flight, one of the twice-daily flights to Miami from Cuba. The waiting list contained one million names. And there was also the chance that her family would suffer if she left. Fidel Castro, the country's leader, often harassed people whose family members escaped.

But she had been playing piano since she was four years old. She'd studied music in college, earning bachelor's and master's degrees from Carlos Alfredo Peyrellade Conservatory. So when her name was miraculously chosen, León said goodbye to her family and boarded the plane alone.

When she arrived in New York City, one of the first people she met was Arthur Mitchell. Mitchell was the first African American principal dancer at the New York City Ballet.

"One day Arthur said to me, 'Why don't you write a piece and I will do the choreography?'" she remembered. "The whole experience moved me so much that I wanted to change my major to composition."

After that first composition, León became a founding member and musical director for the Dance Theater of Harlem. She has since composed an opera, more than 30 pieces of chamber music, a dozen choral pieces, and many orchestral works.

She has conducted orchestras across the world. León has taught at Brooklyn College in New York City since 1985.

In León's music, bird calls flit in and out, bounced along by Caribbean rhythms. She has given bold, operatic voices to the Little Rock Nine, a group of children who were the first to integrate an Arkansas school in the 1960s. And though she rarely sees her family in Cuba, she can hold them close when she makes music. "The third movement, 'Tumbao,'" she says, speaking of one of her compositions, "refers to my father's way of walking—very happy from the heart."

The whole experience moved me so much that I wanted to change my major to composition.
—Tania León

Tania León was nominated for a Grammy Award in 2012 for Best Contemporary Classical Composition.

Chapter 4

NEEDLE AND THREAD

In a museum in Normandy, France, hangs a 900-year-old linen. The Bayeux Tapestry shows more than 70 scenes from the history of ancient Britain. Cavalries, castles, swords, and thrones—vividly captured in colored yarn.

Historians have different ideas about who ordered the artwork, but they agree on one thing: The Bayeux Tapestry was embroidered by women artists who knew the wool they worked as well as the linen background.

The women discussed here also make art out of cloth. Fashion designers make clothing for royalty and everyone else.

Costume designers bring characters and settings to life for moviegoers. And textile artists sew scenes that capture the human experience using needle and thread, just as the Bayeux embroiderers did.

Edith Head
(1897–1981)

Pity the animals of Searchlight, a tiny mining town in Nevada. Cats, dogs, horned toads, mules—just about any creature that held still long enough was dressed in doll

In addition to dressing many of Hollywood's top stars—including Grace Kelly, Paul Newman, John Wayne, and Elizabeth Taylor—Edith Head became a recognizable celebrity in her own right. Her unique personality was also marked by her distinct glasses and short, dark hair.

clothes and decked with ribbons. Edith Head had a costume for everyone.

When she was 14 years old, her parents divorced. Her mother whisked her away to Los Angeles. After graduating from college, Head applied for a job as a sketch artist at Paramount Studios. It was a bold move, since the only art training she had was a few night classes at Chouinard Art College in Los Angeles. When the studio asked to see her work, she showed them drawings her classmates—who dared her to interview—had loaned her. Head got the job. And, even though her employer found out the truth on the first day of work, she kept it.

Head's first project was designing candy-themed costumes for a film. It was disastrous. She used real candy, which melted easily and made a sticky mess in the dancers' hair. Fortunately, she was a fast learner. By the 1930s, she was one of the top designers in Hollywood.

It wasn't long until her costume designs were being nominated for Academy Awards. "If it's a Paramount film I probably designed it," she said later. She also worked for major studios such as Universal Studios, MGM, and Columbia.

SEWING FOR SUFFRAGE

It took nearly 100 years for women to gain the right to vote in national elections in the U.S. Women wrote articles and held rallies for their cause. They marched in parades and protests. Many were beaten and jailed. Along the way, their creativity with cloth helped spread their message.

Historian Ann Bausum writes, "Cloth was a fitting choice. It was a substance all women knew intimately, having woven, sewn, cleaned, and mended it for generations. It was readily available, and everyone knew how to use it. Women turned it into sashes, made it into signs, and sewed it into flags."

She designed costumes for 58 years.

In total, Head was nominated for 34 Academy Awards, and she won eight times—more than any other costume designer in Hollywood history. She also wrote a syndicated advice column to give women fashion tips. The most glamorous stars in Hollywood sought her help. She received her own star on the Hollywood Walk of Fame in 1974.

Her book, *The Dress Doctor*, was published in 1959. Her fashion advice is arranged from A to Z. She shared her experiences working with the biggest stars in the classic era of Hollywood.

Incredibly, her career with Paramount Studios often involved dressing up animals. It was the elephants who objected the most. "Nobody told me that elephants eat leaves. We had great blankets of flowers and grapes, and we made leglets of roses to go around the elephants' legs. The elephant just took up his trunk and ate practically everything."

French fashion designer Coco Chanel in 1926. Chanel helped revolutionize women's fashion by creating stylish and comfortable clothing.

Coco Chanel
(1883–1971)

Gabrielle "Coco" Chanel may have been bored growing up among nuns in a French convent—but she owed her fashion career

Two-toned slingback shoes, tweed suits, the 2.55 quilted handbag (designed in February of 1955—hence the name of the bag), and Chanel No. 5 are some of Chanel's signature items.

to them. After her mother died, her father sent her to a French orphanage. The nuns, in their stark black and white habits, taught the young girl how to sew.

Chanel left the convent as a teenager and went to work for a tailor. One boyfriend helped her start a hat-making business. A later one helped her expand from hats to clothing. She could not afford to sew with lavish fabrics. Instead, she chose inexpensive cloth, such as jersey, which was used to make men's underwear. In Chanel's able hands, it was transformed into couture.

Later style writers described Chanel's designs as a "poor look" or a "poor girl look." Her simple, bold, stylish, yet comfortable clothing was adored by a new generation of women anxious to cast aside formal clothing in order to work and play in a changing society. In 1926, her iconic

"little black dress" appeared on the cover of *Vogue.* By the late 1920s, the Chanel line included clothing, textiles, perfume, and jewelry.

Despite her success, there was a period when her style could not make up for her politics. Early in World War II, Chanel fell in love with a Nazi officer. She is said to have spied for the Germans during the war. Chanel also held views about Jewish people that are widely considered anti-Semitic. After the war, she was disgraced.

Despite the public scorn, she kept working. During the 1950s and 1960s, her designs made a comeback. First Lady Jacqueline Kennedy was a fan of Chanel's slim suits and pillbox hats. Audrey Hepburn wore one of Chanel's "little black dresses" in the film *Breakfast At Tiffany's* (1961). In the 1990s, Princess Diana was seen wearing Chanel. By the time Chanel died, her reputation had bounced back from the war years. Today, she is regarded as perhaps the most popular fashion designer of the 20th century.

Faith Ringgold
(1930-)

In Faith Ringgold's childhood home in Harlem, New York, she was surrounded by stories. During the 1930s and 1940s, her family members were moving up from the south in a steady stream. Ringgold remembered, "As children we were so happy to see them as they were constantly telling stories about their adventures."

Art was also a big part of Ringgold's life. Because she had asthma, she was often home

In 1999, Faith Ringgold began her Coming to Jones Road series. Each story quilt told the story of slaves escaping on the Underground Railroad.

with her mother, who was a seamstress. She played with fabric scraps and painting supplies while her mother sewed. She never wanted to be anything other than an artist when she grew up.

Ringgold graduated from the City College of New York in 1959, the first woman and first African American to study there. She taught art in public schools while working on a master's degree. She created some powerful works of art, including a series of paintings called "American People" that confronted racism in society. During the 1960s, she staged protests to call attention to the fact that museums showcased very few women artists or artists of color. Once, she was even jailed for protesting.

Ringgold toured Europe to explore new art forms. She created *thangka* paintings inspired by those created in Tibet. She made masks inspired by African works of art.

Some of her most famous pieces were what she called "story quilts." These were fabric quilts that depicted autobiographical scenes along with written text.

One story quilt is called "Tar Beach." After seeing the quilt, Andrea Cascardi, a children's book editor, helped Ringgold incorporate the scenes in the quilt into a picture book. *Tar Beach* has been a best-selling book for over 25 years.

Faith Ringgold created more than a dozen picture books. Many of her other works of art are housed in museums all over the world. She has been honored with a National Endowment for the Arts Award, a Guggenheim Fellowship, and an NAACP Image Award.

Thangka paintings are made with ground pigments. The pigments are brushed onto fabric. Thangka paintings often feature Buddhist deities.

Ruth Carter

(1960–)

Ruth Carter grew up in a household with five brothers, so she was no stranger to comic book heroes. But she could not have guessed back then that the fictional world of Wakanda would become part of her real life. In 2019, Carter won the Academy Award for Best Costume Design for her work on the record-breaking Marvel movie *Black Panther*.

By the time she received the award, she had designed costumes for more than 40 movies. She began with Spike Lee's *School Daze* in 1988. She worked with Lee on four other films, including the Oscar-winning film *Malcom X*. Carter has designed costumes for some of Hollywood's most respected

In 2019, Ruth Carter became the first African American to win an Oscar for costume design.

> *I feel like I've been designing superheroes my whole life. Malcolm X was a superhero. Tina Turner was a superhero. Martin Luther King was a superhero.*
>
> —Ruth Carter

directors and actors, including Steven Spielberg, Oprah Winfrey, and Denzel Washington.

Part of the reason her costumes resonate with audiences is that they are authentic. She travels the world to search through historic archives and source material. Carter also treats other cultures with deep respect. For example, when she wanted to weave tribal designs into some *Black Panther* costumes, her team traveled to the African kingdom of Lesotho to get permission from Basotho people first.

For those who understand the fine art of costume design, that makes Carter a superhero. "I just want people to look at my films for now and forever more and know that I was a keeper of the culture," she says.

YARNSTORMING THE CITY

IIn 2005, Magda Sayeg got an idea. What if she could make the things around her prettier with yarn? She knitted a cover for her shop's doorknob, and yarnstorming was born. Trees, statues, fences, and other public spaces were decorated with brightly colored yarn.

In 2009, Lauren O'Farrell—also known as Deadly Knitshade—and several creative friends began telling "stitched stories." The artists created knitted or crocheted

Yarnstorming is also known as yarn bombing, urban knitting, and graffiti knitting.

toylike characters to fit a theme or a story. Then they were displayed in public spaces around London for everyone to enjoy. O'Farrell called her project Knit the City.

Chapter 5

LENS AND LIGHT

Today, photos can be snapped, altered, and posted within a matter of minutes. But photographers as early as last century worked very differently.

Camera lenses were long or short, and carried in separate cases. Cameras contained film that had to be developed in dark rooms—bathed in liquid chemicals and hung up to dry.

The women discussed here saw the world they lived in through a unique lens. They made artistic portraits and surrealist compositions. They documented migrations, wars, revolutions, and elections—in addition to taking the occasional selfie.

Dorothea Lange
(1895–1965)

In 1929, the United States fell into a financial depression when the stock market crashed. This was followed by a major drought. Dust storms blew across the land. American farmers were devastated.

These desperate conditions drew Dorothea Lange out of her studio and onto the road. A survivor of childhood polio,

Dorothea Lange is known for her images of people hit hard by the crash of the stock market and the dust storms that swept across the western plains of the United States in the 1930s.

she understood something about suffering. She said, "[It] was the most important thing that happened to me, and formed me, guided me, instructed me, helped me, and humiliated me." Her familiarity with pain shows up in her photography.

Lange traveled the western United States while working for government relief agencies. She believed her art had a purpose beyond beauty. She photographed people waiting in bread lines, as well as traveling soap sellers, lumber workers, sharecroppers, and migrant farmers. She recorded what their living conditions were like. When government officials saw Lange's work, they sent people to investigate and help.

Lange's most iconic photograph is now known as *Migrant Mother.* One day, she drove past a farm where migrant families picked peas. She came across Florence Owens Thompson, a mother who had traveled from Oklahoma with her seven children, looking for work. Lange's photograph shows the worry etched into her subject's face.

Lange's respectful, powerful photos turned America's eye toward the poor as few other artists had done before. Policies changed. Money and services flowed to people who needed them.

Lange's photography helped people again during World War II (1939–1945). After Japan bombed Pearl Harbor on December 7, 1941, the U.S. government rounded up Japanese American citizens. They were forced to leave their homes and businesses and live in internment camps for the rest of the war. Lange was there too. Her images were so powerful that the U.S. government kept her photos hidden from the public until 1964. Lange kept taking pictures until her death from cancer in 1965.

"Bad as it is," she said, "the world is potentially full of good photographs. But to be good, photographs have to be full of the world."

Lee Miller (second from right) and five other war correspondents who covered the U.S. Army, 1943

Lee Miller

(1907-1977)

Nineteen-year-old Lee Miller stepped onto a busy Manhattan street. Brakes screeched and a firm hand yanked her to safety just in time. The blonde teenager was saved—remarkably—by the publisher of *Vogue* magazine. He decided then and there to make her a model. Within a few months, Miller was on the cover of *Vogue*.

IT'S MARY BLAIR'S WORLD, AFTER ALL

In Walt Disney's heyday, women were primarily employed to ink in the designs that men made. But there were a few standout female artists Disney relied on for special projects. One was watercolor artist Mary Blair. She had a flair for bright colors and modern geometric design. Disney put her in charge of designing concept art for several movies: *Cinderella* (1950), *Alice in Wonderland* (1951), and *Peter Pan* (1953).

Blair is best known for her dazzling design on the theme park ride "it's a small world." The ride was created for the 1964 World's Fair in New York City. It was moved to Disneyland in California in 1966. Today, visitors to Disney parks in Hong Kong, Tokyo, Orlando, and Paris can hop aboard too. The "it's a small world" ride is considered a Walt Disney masterpiece.

Before long, Miller realized she wanted to be behind the lens, not in front of it. In 1927, she moved to Paris, France, to learn from surrealist photographer Man Ray. Bold and assertive, Miller persuaded Ray to be her mentor. She was an excellent student. By 1930, she had her own studio and was working for some of the most famous fashion designers, including Coco Chanel.

Miller traveled between Paris, New York, and Egypt. She gained fame as a photographer. When World War II began, Miller wanted to photograph the action. She asked British *Vogue* to make her a war correspondent, and they agreed.

Miller followed Allied soldiers. She took daring and often disturbing photographs, and wrote candid stories to go with them. Miller was with the troops when they liberated the concentration camps at the end of the war. Her photographs revealed the war's cruelty.

After the war, Miller put away her camera. What she had seen had taken a toll on her. It was not until after her death from cancer in 1977 that much of her wartime work was discovered in her attic.

Lee Miller's surrealist, commercial, and wartime photographs revealed an artist deeply in touch with the world at a time of rapid change.

Carrie Mae Weems
(1953–)

Carrie Mae Weems danced down the hallways of her grandfather's house in Portland, Oregon. Her dream was to become a professional dancer. When she was 17, she joined the respected San Francisco Dancer's Workshop. But then, when she turned 20, the gift of a camera changed her life.

She traveled to New York City in 1976 and started taking photography classes. When life there did not work out the way she'd planned, she returned to California.

Art critics have said that Weems's photographs explore identity, race, and

Carrie Mae Weems has been featured in rap lyrics, in a Netflix series, and on a book of poetry.

a mother in others. She often places herself in the center of the scene, looking directly at the camera.

"Long before I picked up a camera I was deeply concerned with the ways in which African Americans were depicted," Weems said, "and, for the most part, I didn't like what I saw. So one way of dealing with it was to step in and rethink how black women, more specifically, need to be represented."

In another series, Weems started with images of enslaved people from Harvard University's archives. She took pictures of these old photographs, tinted them red, and paired them with her own writing. The series is titled From Here I Saw What Happened and I Cried. Harvard University threatened to sue. They said she should not have used their images. No lawsuit was ever filed, and today Harvard proudly displays some of the images in its collection.

Her 2007 Museum series features photographs of Weems standing outside

gender. But Weems herself thinks of them as exploring humanity—especially what it is like to love something or someone without being loved back. In her most famous group of photos, The Kitchen Table series, Weems is sitting at—what else?—a kitchen table. She appears with a man in some photographs and with a daughter or

famous art museums. The photographs seem to speak out about what it feels like to love art and yet be excluded from art museums.

"I can spend an evening at most art functions in New York City and not see a single other person of color," she said. "Now. Today. That's shocking to me."

Weems has had more than 50 solo shows in her lifetime. In 2013 she received a MacArthur Fellowship Award and the Congressional Black Caucus Foundation's Lifetime Achievement Award.

Shirin Neshat
(1957–)

Though she has lived in exile for many years, Shirin Neshat vividly recalls her childhood home in Qazvin, Iran. She can see and smell the fruit farm where she walked with her father in spring, when the wind was scented with blossoms.

In 1974, she left home to finish her education in Los Angeles, California. But

Iranian-born artist and filmmaker Shirin Neshat poses in front of her exhibition series Our House is On Fire.

in 1979, there was a revolution. Afterward, women had fewer rights. People who criticized the government were punished harshly. When Neshat returned in 1990, Iran was not a safe place for her to live.

Neshat found a way to tell the world what life was like for women in Iran. She created a series of photographs called Women of Allah. Veiled women hold weapons. On their faces, hands, and feet, Neshat wrote poetry in Farsi, the language spoken in Iran. She was exploring the kinds of power Iranian women had and did not have in the post-revolution culture. Not everybody saw her vision when they were shown in a New York gallery in 1994. Some people thought she was praising violence.

Neshat responded, "Everything I have ever done has generated a lot of debate, and not all of it has been praise."

Next, Neshat began to use moving images in her art. In *Turbulence*, she used two giant video screens. On one screen, a man sings an ancient Persian song for an audience. On the other, a woman sings a song without words, alone in an empty room. Women are forbidden to sing in public in Iran. The project won the top award at the 1999 Venice Biennale, one of the world's most respected art exhibitions.

Neshat continues to explore what it is like to live as an Iranian woman in a repressive culture and as an artist in exile. In the garden of her New York home, there are cherry and lemon trees. It may not be the same fragrance that drifted through the orchards of her childhood, but it is beautiful in its own way.

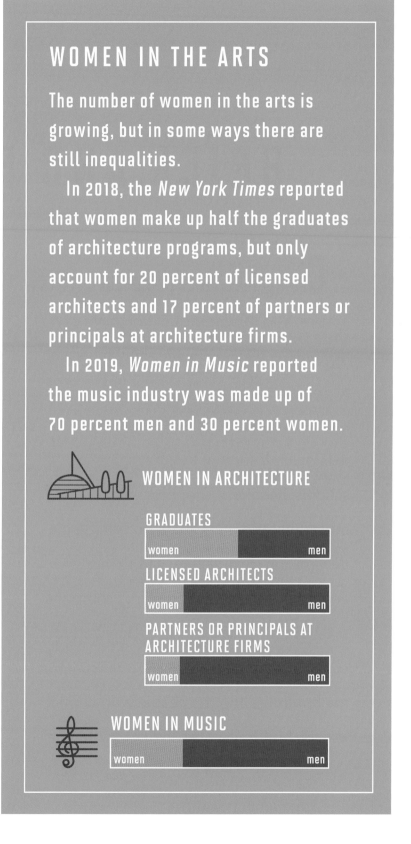

WOMEN IN THE ARTS

The number of women in the arts is growing, but in some ways there are still inequalities.

In 2018, the *New York Times* reported that women make up half the graduates of architecture programs, but only account for 20 percent of licensed architects and 17 percent of partners or principals at architecture firms.

In 2019, *Women in Music* reported the music industry was made up of 70 percent men and 30 percent women.

WOMEN IN ARCHITECTURE

GRADUATES

women | men

LICENSED ARCHITECTS

women | men

PARTNERS OR PRINCIPALS AT ARCHITECTURE FIRMS

women | men

WOMEN IN MUSIC

women | men

Chapter 6

BRICK AND BLUEPRINTS

Calling all builders of blanket forts, tree houses, and sandcastles. If you have ever designed a play space, you may have a bit of architect in you.

The women discussed here have designed all sorts of buildings: homes, schools, hospitals, shopping malls, museums, and memorials. To bring their designs into reality, they had to master geometry, algebra, engineering, computer programming, and physics. They had to work with the people who would construct the buildings and the people who would use the buildings. On top of everything else, these architects had to make the practical and functional beautiful.

Dame Jane Drew
(1911–1996)

Every night it was the same: first, the faraway drone of plane engines. Then sirens. Then people racing to take shelter as the German Luftwaffe (air force) bombed the city of London. Many people in London—especially those living in the borough of Hackney—owed their safety to the network of air raid shelters designed by architect Jane Drew. She designed more than 11,000 of the underground bunkers. Drew's own offices were destroyed in the war, but her work saved thousands of lives.

Dame Jane Drew had a long and successful career as a modernist architect and town planner.

Those bunkers were not the only civil service Drew performed. After graduating from the Architectural Association School of Architecture in 1934 and opening her own all-female architecture firm, Drew accepted a post in Ghana, West Africa, in 1947. Working with the British Colonial Office, Drew and her husband, Maxwell Fry, designed schools, hospitals, and public buildings. Drew was known for talking to the local people—often in their own languages, which she took the time to learn—as part of the design process.

She specialized in tropical modernism—a design style that used local materials and climate-friendly open spaces. Her design manual, *Village Housing in the Tropics* (1947), was written to help local villagers build their own spaces using the principles of tropical modernism.

Drew spent much of her career designing buildings outside of England. She designed buildings on the campus of the University of Ibadan in Nigeria from 1949 to 1960. One of her most famous projects was the planned city of Chandigarh, India. She also worked in Sri Lanka, Iran, and Singapore. When she returned to England, she designed hospitals and public housing.

Her modernist designs were bold and striking. But for Jane Drew, a beautiful design was only one aim. She loved making sure people had access to healthcare, housing, and educational spaces.

Zaha Hadid
(1950–2016)

Zaha Hadid could follow her memories back to the trip that inspired her to become an architect. She was 11 years old. Her father had taken her to see the Sumerian cities near her home in Baghdad, Iraq. These were some of the very first structures ever built by human beings.

They explored the marshland of the Tigris and Euphrates rivers. "We went by boat, and then on a smaller one made of

Zaha Hadid poses in front of the Pheano Science Center Museum in Wolfsburg, Germany. The impressive concrete building was designed by Hadid and her firm and opened to the public in 2005.

schools in England and Switzerland. White there, she studied math and architecture in Lebanon. She opened her own architectural firm in 1979.

As an architect, Hadid drew for years before any of her designs were constructed. People thought it would be impossible to build her swooping, diving, swirling drawings.

Some called her a "paper architect" because her works never moved beyond sketches. Some of her designs were so beautiful they were hung in museums.

Finally, in 1993, her design for the Vitra Fire Station in Germany was built. Next, she planned the light-filled MAXXI Museum in Italy. Gradually, her buildings became curvier, like the eddies

reeds, to visit villages in the marshes," she told *The Guardian* newspaper. "The beauty of the landscape—where sand, water, reeds, birds, buildings and people all somehow flowed together—has never left me."

Hadid's parents sent her to boarding

In 2019, The Serpentine Gallery, a London museum space designed by Zaha Hadid, hosted an exhibition of the art of Faith Ringgold.

in a river or a reed bending in a coastal breeze. She imagined buildings in all sorts of shapes, made of unusual materials, all over the world.

In 2004, Hadid was the first woman to receive the Pritzker Prize in Architecture. She was also the first to receive the United Kingdom's highest architectural award, the Stirling Prize, in 2010 and 2011. In 2016, she became the only woman to receive the Royal Gold Medal from the Royal Institute of British Architects.

Until the end of her life, landscapes continued to inspire her. "Some winters ago, I flew from New York to Chicago in the snow," she said, "At sunset, the landscape and cityscapes became no colors other than starkly contrasted black and white, while the rivers and lakes were blood red. Amazing. You wouldn't call that a nice landscape, but it had the quality of light and life I would love to get into our buildings."

Maya Lin
(1959–)

What began as a class project became the most visited war memorial in the United States. Maya Lin, a 20-year-old college student at the time, entered a contest for the design of the Vietnam Veterans Memorial in Washington, D.C., in 1981. Her entry was unusual: a v-shaped polished glass wall embedded in the ground. The smooth black glass was to be engraved with the names of all 58,000 service members of the U.S. armed forces who were killed in the Vietnam War.

When the design was chosen from among the 1,400 other entries, Lin was shocked. It had only scored a "B" at school. Lin's idea sparked a controversy. Some felt that having the wall partially buried in the earth implied a sense of shame about the war. Others did not like its color, saying black was the color of sorrow.

For Lin, the Vietnam Veterans Memorial was the first of many architectural designs that brought people into closer contact with the earth. Her design for the Civil Rights Memorial in Montgomery, Alabama, is all about water. Sheets of water pour over a black granite cone. The memorial features a quote Dr. Martin Luther King Jr. used in his "I Have a Dream" speech. Etched into the stone are the words "Until justice rolls down like water and righteousness like a mighty stream." That quote originated in the book of Amos in the Bible. The granite cone is engraved with the names of 41 people killed in the struggle for civil rights in the United States.

Lin has made more than memorials. In 1995, she created *Wave Field*, a sculpture at the University of Michigan in Ann Arbor. It is made up of 6-foot (1.8 m) tall grass-covered mounds shaped like waves.

One of her largest works is called the *Confluence Project*. It is a series of seven outdoor installations along the Columbia

Maya Lin received the Presidential Medal of Freedom from President Barack Obama on November 22, 2016.

and Snake rivers in Washington and Oregon. The project deals with the journey of early American explorers Meriwether Lewis and William Clark, who charted a path across the continent to the Pacific

Ocean. Lin's artwork explores the effects Lewis and Clark's journey eventually had on Native American communities in the region. The word *confluence* means the place where rivers run together, and the project speaks to the ways cultures also come together.

In 2009, President Barack Obama gave Lin the National Medal of Arts, and in 2016, he awarded her the Presidential Medal of Freedom.

Kazuyo Sejima
(1954–)

What Kazuyo Sejima wanted, when she was young, was to be a grandmother.

"They are relaxed," she said. In the words of her design partner, Ryue Nishizawa, Sejima wanted to "sit on the terrace and enjoy the sunlight."

Sejima has accomplished part of that early dream. Her architectural designs allow room for lots of sunlight. Glass exterior walls allow people to feel they are part of the natural world, even when they are inside. In one memorable building, the New Museum in New York City, Sejima and Nishizawa stacked different size floors on top of one another. They staggered the placement so they could create skylights and terraces. People might enjoy seeing some of the art outside, they thought. And the skylights would allow the sun to illuminate the artist's work.

Sejima's career as an architect began after she graduated from Japan Women's University in Tokyo in 1981. For several years, she worked for a respected architect named Toyo Ito. In 1987, she established her own architectural firm. She and Nishizawa

Kazuyo Sejima posses with her design partner, Ryue Nishizawa, as they unveil their Serpentine Gallery Pavilion in London, on July 8, 2009.

joined forces in 1995. The union allowed them to tackle larger projects.

These projects can be seen all over the world. Sejima's open, organic, and sometimes geometric designs have transformed the way people interact inside her structures.

"I have a dream that architecture can bring something to contemporary society," she says. "Architecture is how people meet in space."

Women throughout time and across the world have created countless works of art. And they have created something else: opportunity. Because of their courage and creativity, the world now knows that art is for everyone.

Timeline

1896 Nampeyo paints ancient Hopi designs onto her pottery.

1905 Camille Claudel creates *L'Abandon*, which draws both praise and scandal.

1925 Frida Kahlo is injured and starts painting during her long recovery.

1926 Coco Chanel's "little black dress" makes the cover of *Vogue* magazine.

1935 The Federal Art Program is founded through the WPA, leading to the creation of 200,000 works of public art.

1936 Dorothea Lange takes her famous *Migrant Mother* photograph.

1937 Martha Graham is invited to perform at the White House.

1938 Katherine Dunham produces her first ballet, *L'Ag'Ya*, which debuts in Chicago.

1939 Augusta Savage completes *The Harp* for the 1939 World's Fair in New York City.

1945 Lee Miller sends photographs of the concentration camps to her editors at *Vogue*.

1947 Dame Jane Drew publishes *Village Housing in the Tropics*.

1949 Edith Head wins an Academy Award for Best Costume Design for *The Emperor Waltz*.

1962 Marisol Escobar debuts her signature life-size sculptures at the Stable Gallery.

1964 Mary Blair's "it's a small world" ride opens at the World's Fair in New York.

1969 Tania León becomes the first music director at the Dance Theater of Harlem.

1973 Carrie Mae Weems starts snapping photographs.

1977 Georgia O'Keeffe is awarded the Presidential Medal of Freedom.

1979 Judy Chicago's *The Dinner Party*, opens at the San Francisco Museum of Modern Art.

1981 Maya Lin's design is chosen for the Vietnam Veterans Memorial.

1986 Lubaina Himid's first solo show, *A Fashionable Marriage*, opens in London.

1992 Faith Ringgold's book *Tar Beach* wins the Caldecott Medal for illustration.

1993 Zaha Hadid's *Vitra Fire Station* is constructed in Weil am Rhein, Germany.

1994 Shirin Neshat's photography exhibit, *Women of Allah*, opens in New York City.

2015 Alma Thomas's *Resurrection* becomes the first painting by an African American artist to be included in the permanent art collection at the White House.

2017 The Yayoi Kusama Museum opens in Tokyo, Japan.

2018 Kazuyo Sejima designs express trains for Seibu Railway in Japan.

2019 Ruth Carter wins the Academy Award for Best Costume Design for *Black Panther*.

Source Notes

p. 4, "Do your work…" Ivy Storvick, "The Interview: Faith Ringgold," *Matches Fashion, 2019*, matchesfashion.com/us/womens/the-style-report/2019/06/the-poolside-style-issue/the-interview-faith-ringgold-artist-aw19 Accessed January 30, 2020.

p. 8, "But it was all academic." Georgia O'Keeffe, "A Life in Art," (3:28), youtube.com/watch?v=NV1w0IK_sdA Accessed January 30, 2020.

p. 8, "So what ?..." Georgia O'Keeffe, "The Life of an Artist," (12:02), youtube.com/watch?v=NV1w0IK_sdA Accessed January 30, 2020.

p. 11, "Color is life…" Smithsonian American Art Museum, "Alma Thomas profile," americanart.si.edu/artist/alma-thomas-4778 Accessed January 30, 2020.

p. 11, "One of the things…" Peter Schjeldahl, "Alma Thomas's Late Blooms," *The New Yorker*, July 18, 2016, newyorker.com/magazine/2016/07/25/alma-thomas-and-sports-photography Accessed January 30, 2020.

p. 14, "Our Earth is only…" TATE profile, "Who is Yayoi Kusama?" tate.org.uk/kids/explore/who-is/who-yayoi-kusama Accessed January 30, 2020.

p. 14, "My mother was a textile designer…" Sophia Bennett and Manjit Thapp, "Getting to Know Lubaina Himid," *TATE*, March 26, 2019, www.tate.org.uk/art/artists/lubaina-himid-2356/getting-know-lubaina-himid Accessed January 30, 2020.

p. 15, "If you don't see yourself..." Lubaina Himid: "I Am Painting Parts of Black Women's Lives That Nobody Paints," *Vogue*, March 6, 2018, www.vogue.co.uk/article/lubaina-himid-interview Accessed February 17, 2020.

p. 18, "When I first…" Barbara Kramer. *Nampeyo and Her Pottery*. Tucson, AZ: The University of Arizona Press, 1996, p. 28.

p. 20, "My father…" Smithsonian American Art Museum, "Augusta Savage profile," 2019, americanart.si.edu/artist/augusta-savage-4269, Accessed January 30, 2020.

p. 22, "I was very sad myself…" Sebastian Smee, "Revisiting Marisol, Years After Her Heyday," *The Boston Globe*, July 5, 2014, bostonglobe.com/arts/theater-art/2014/07/05/red-hot-now-little-known-great-artist-marisol-being-rediscovered/DluCcPEdkzosTUcjud1swI/story.html Accessed January 30, 2020.

p. 24, "All anybody wants…" Jem Aswad, "Billie Eilish and Her Brother and Co-Writer, Finneas, Get Deep About Their Music and What's Next." *Variety*. December 4, 2019, variety.com/2019/music/news/billie-eilish-finneas-oconnell-songwriting-1203421768/Accessed January 30, 2020.

p. 26, "I have never gone to..." Eugene Gates, "Mrs. H. H. A. Beach: American Symphonist," *The Kapralova Society Journal, Volume 8, Issue 2 (Fall 2010),* kapralova.org/journal15.pdf Accessed January 30, 2020.

p. 26, "One thing I have learned..." "Ibid., Accessed January 30, 2020.

p. 26, "What do you see?" Ellen O'Connell Whittet, "How Like the Mind It Is," *The Paris Review*, July 16, 2018, theparisreview.org/blog/2018/07/16/how-like-the-mind-it-is/, Accessed February 17, 2020.

p. 28, "You are in competition..." The Martha Graham Dance Company, 1957, "A Dancers World," (13:40), youtube.com/watch?v=aFTNmGBKC2Y Accessed January 30, 2020.

p. 30, "One day Arthur said..." "Tania LeÓn: Diversity in Composing and Life," *American Federation of Musicians*, afm.org/2018/02/tania-leon-diversity-composing-life/ Accessed February 18, 2020.

p. 31, "The third movement..." Ibid. Accessed February 18, 2020.

p. 31, "The whole experience..." Ibid. Accessed February 18, 2020.

p. 34, "Cloth was a fitting choice..." Ann Bausum. *With Courage and Cloth: Winning the Fight for a Woman's Right to Vote*. Washington, D.C.: National Geographic, 2004, p. 9.

p. 35, "Nobody told me..." Jay Jorgensen. *Edith Head: The Fifty-Year Career of Hollywood's Greatest Costume Designer*. New York: Lifetime Media, 2010, p. 29.

p. 37, "As children..." Ivy Storvik, "The Interview: Faith Ringgold," *Matches Fashion*, matchesfashion.com/us/womens/the-style-report/2019/06/the-poolside-style-issue/the-interview-faith-ringgold-artist-aw19 Accessed February 18, 2020.

p. 40, "I feel like..." Alice Newbold, "Why Black Panther's Costumes Break the Superhero Mould," *Vogue*, February 9, 2018, vogue.co.uk/article/black-panther-costume-designer-ruth-e-carter Accessed February 18, 2020.

p. 40, "I just want..." Michelle Darrisaw, "The Powerful Message Black Panther's Costume Designer (and Oscar Winner) Ruth E. Carter Wants to Send Through Clothing," *The Oprah Magazine*, Feruary 25, 2019, oprahmag.com/entertainment/tv-movies/a26339364/ruth-carter-black-panther-costumes-interview/ Accessed February 18, 2020.

p. 44, "Bad as it is…" Museum of Modern Art (MoMA) profile "Dorothea Lange, American (1895–1965)," 2018, moma.org/artists/3373?locale=en, Accessed January 30, 2020.

p. 47, "Long before…" Diane Solway, "Mary J. Blige and Carrie Mae Weems in Conversation: On Race, Women, Music and the Future," *W Magazine*, November 6, 2017, wmagazine.com/story/mary-j-blige-mudbound-carrie-mae-weems-photographs-w-magazine-art-issue Accessed January 30, 2020.

p. 48,"I can spend…" Hilarie M. Sheets, "Photographer and Subject are One," *The New York Times*, September 12, 2012, nytimes.com/2012/09/16/arts/design/carrie-mae-weems-photographer-and-subject.html Accessed January 30, 2020.

p. 49, "Everything I have done..." Cristina Ruiz, "Shirin Nestat," *The Gentlewoman*, Spring & Summer 2018, thegentlewoman.co.uk/library/shirin-neshat Accessed February 10, 2020.

p. 52, "Then we went by boat…" Jonathan Glancey, "I Don't Do Nice," *The Guardian*, October 9, 2006, theguardian.com/artanddesign/2006/oct/09/architecture.communities Accessed January 30, 2020.

p. 54, "Some winters ago..." Ibid. Accessed February 15, 2020.

p. 56, "They are relaxed…" Designboom, October, 29, 2005, "SANNA: kazuyo sejima + ryue nishizawa: designboom interview," designboom.com/interviews/sanaa-kazuyo-sejima-ryue-nishizawa-designboom-interview/ Accessed January 30, 2020.

p. 57, "I have…" Caroline Roux, "Kazuyo Sejima: She can foresee the future of architecture," *The Gentlewoman*, Issue no. 1: Spring/Summer 2010, thegentlewoman.co.uk/library/kazuyo-sejima , Accessed January 30, 2020.

Select Bibliography

Beach, Amy. Music Division, Library of Congress. loc.gov/item/ihas.200153246/ Accessed January 30, 2020.

Das, Joanna Dee. *Katherine Dunham: Dance and the African Diaspora*. New York: Oxford University Press, 2017.

Gates, Eugene. "Mrs. H. H. A. Beach: American Symphonist," *The Kapralova Society Journal, Volume 8, Issue 2 (Fall 2010)*, kapralova.org/journal15.pdf

Jackson, Iaian. "Jane Drew (1911–1996)," *Architectural Review,* July 4, 2014, architectural-review.com/essays/reputations/jane-drew-1911-1996/8665224.article Accessed January 30, 2020.

Jorgenson, Jay. *Edith Head: The Fifty Year Career of Hollywood's Greatest Costume Designer*. Philadelphia, PA: Running Press, 2010.

Kramer, Barbara. *Nampeyo and Her Works*. Tucson, AZ: The University of Arizona Press, 1996.

Kusama, Yayoi. *Infinity Net*. Tate Publishing, 2013.

Latson, Jennifer. "How Poverty Shaped Coco Chanel," *Time*, August 19, 2015, time.com/3994196/coco-chanel-1883/ Accessed January 30, 2020.

Risner, Vicky J. "Katherina Dunham: A Life in Dance," *Library of Congress Performing Arts Encyclopedia*. loc.gov/item/ihas.200152685/ Accessed January 30, 2020.

Stramberg, Susan. "Sculptor Augusta Savage Said Her Legacy Was The Work Of Her Students." *National Public Radio,* July 15, 2109. npr.org/2019/07/15/740459875/sculptor-augusta-savage-said-her-legacy-was-the-work-of-her-students Accessed January 30, 2020.

Waldrep, Carolyn, ed. *By a Woman's Hand: Illustrators of the Golden Age*. Mineola, NY: Dover Publishing, Inc.

About the Author

Rebecca Stanborough obtained her BA from Agnes Scott College, a women's college in Decatur, Georgia. She also earned an MFA in Writing for Children and Adults from Minnesota's Hamline University. Rebecca is the author of four other books for young readers, and her short story "The Latter Days of Jean" appeared in the Capstone anthology Love & Profanity. She writes and teaches in St. Augustine, Florida.

Glossary

abstract—an art term used to describe a work of art that does not represent or look like something else

anthropologist—a scientist who studies human cultures and traditions

beeweed—a grass that, when boiled, makes a dark syrup that can be blended with pigments to make paint

concentration camp—a camp where people such as prisoners of war, political prisoners, or refugees are held

couture—fashionable clothing that is custom-made

deconstructionism—an art term used to explain how a work of art is better understood by looking at its parts

diaspora—when people leave their homeland and move to other places in the world

drought—a period when little or no rain falls

egg tempera—an ancient paint made by blending pigments with a thick binding liquid, usually the yolk of an egg

exile—when a person is not allowed to return to their native country

Great Depression—a period in the 1930s when the stock market in the U.S. crashed, leading to a decade-long period of severe economic hardship for many Americans

indigenous—someone or something that is native to a particular region

integrate—to bring together people of different races and backgrounds

plein air—an art term used to describe painting outdoors

repressive—a society or political system that restrains a person or group's freedom

surrealist—an art term that refers to art that relies on images lifted from the subconscious mind of the artist and that have a dream-like quality

theocracy—a form of government where a country's civil leaders are guided by the dominant religion

Critical Thinking Questions

1. Critics say that Carrie Mae Weems's photographs explore race, identity, and gender. Weems herself, though, says her focus is on humanity, and how it feels to love without being loved in return. Find some of her photographs online and see whether you agree with the critics or with Weems. Support your answer with examples either from this book or in your online research.
2. Some of the artists in this book work with pottery, baskets, yarn, and fabric—things we often associate with home. Art critics sometimes downgrade art made with these materials, calling it "crafts" rather than "fine art." Should critics separate art into these categories? How might these categories affect the respect we give to artists who work with these materials?
3. The artists in this book came from many different backgrounds. Name some characteristics that many of these women have in common.

Further Reading

Bennett, Sophia and Manjit Thapp. *The Bigger Picture: Women Who Changed the Art World*. London: Tate Publishing, 2019.

Ignatofsky, Rachel. *Women in the Arts: 50 Fearless Creatives Who Inspired the World*. Berkeley, CA: Ten Speed Press, 2019.

Johnson, Mindy. *Pencils, Pens & Brushes: A Great Girls' Guide to Disney Animation*. New York: Disney Press, 2019.

Internet Sites

Modern Women: Women Artists at the Museum of Modern Art
https://www.moma.org/interactives/modern_women/

National Museum of Women in the Arts
https://nmwa.org/

National Women's History Museum
https://www.womenshistory.org/

Index